The Sky Is Not the Limit

Robert O. Fisch

NODIN PRESS

ISBN 978-0-9679746-2-0
Library of Congress Control Number: 2013943806

Published by
Nodin Press
5114 Cedar Lake Road
Minneapolis, MN 55416

The Sky Is Not the Limit

In memory of
my beloved parents, Zoltán and Irén Fisch,
and my dear governess, Anna Tátrai.

To my daughter, Alex, my wife, Karen,
and my friends with love.

My thanks to Norton Stillman and many of my friends for their help in making this book a reality, especially Lynne Thompson for keen editorial support and insightful advice and Ann Benrud for early assistance.

And deep gratitude to William McGuire for writing the foreword that brings clarity and perspective to this book's purpose.

Contents

Foreword

We live in a world of amazing accomplishment and progress. It is also a time of great uncertainty as we confront evil alongside good, violence disrupting peace, startling economic disparities, bias of all types and forces that seek to suppress the very essence of the human spirit. We will need the best of every individual in our society if we are to successfully overcome the challenges of these circumstances.

The Sky Is Not the Limit provides us a pathway to this end. Within these pages is the wisdom of a man who has displayed, in many different but equally profound ways, the pinnacle of the human spirit. Dr. Robert O. Fisch has balanced the good and the bad, the controllable with the uncontrollable, the planned and the unforeseen, and emerged at a place of personal peace and public sharing. For him, each new day becomes the best day of his life. He acknowledges the immense personal value of art, music, education, nature, all cultures and the act of helping others. He is centered on the virtues of humankind, the glories and wonders of life and our world, and the unlimited potential of individual aspiration.

Why listen to this particular voice? It is because of the profound way Robert Fisch has conducted himself through the challenges and opportunities of eighty-eight years, and the straightforward, practical counsel he offers us today. It is a privilege to have so intimate a glimpse into such a life, and to have the opportunity to apply lessons from it to our own.

I recall a lunch with Robert when, while enjoying a French baguette (his favorite part of every meal), he confided that he later grew to appreciate those months living with hunger and death in a Nazi concentration camp. His explanation was that the suffering allowed him to appreciate every opportunity and blessing in life. For him, bad experiences taught invaluable lessons, which in turn became part of his own being and moral compass. Each minute of life is viewed as a gift, and it is his hope that all individuals will reach their fullest potential while showing compassion, understanding and love.

Actor George Chakiris said, "No matter how dark the moment, love and hope are always possible." Robert Fisch has taken that notion many steps further, providing us lessons on how to expand and optimize our own lives. He reminds us that we don't need a personal counselor or psychologist to get there; we simply need to adjust our thinking and embrace the power and joy of our being.

After reading Fisch's first book, *Light from the Yellow Star*, a young girl wrote to him to share her thoughts. She alluded to her own personal tragedies and said how, unlike fairy-tale endings in Disney movies, her experiences often ended in tears, pain and even death. She then expressed hope that there still could be occasional "Happily Ever After" experiences. From that young heart came some telling words about Robert Fisch.

"You, Dr. Fisch, are a Happily Ever After. You have overcome being hated, oppressed, and one of the most horrific events in human history. You've overcome that. Now look at you! You're a knight, an artist, a writer, and an old man. In some countries, just being elderly would be a pretty good achievement. You have books published, a family that loves you and I'm sure you have a nice house...you, Dr. Fisch, are a Happily Ever After."

In *The Sky Is Not the Limit*, we meet this person through relevant, at times quirky and often sardonic thoughts that spring from him as easily as his broad smile and guttural laugh. Here is the wisdom of a life that repeatedly shows us the meaning of resilience, the value behind the search for good and the heights to which we may aspire. Through words that at times read like proverbs, he has drawn from his own life experience to offer practical advice along with answers to important questions. Further, while providing ideas that clearly relate to the necessities of the day-to-day, he offers insight into more fundamental aspects of personal growth and our inner being. For instance, how do we take a web of experiences—both good and bad—and translate them into a good life?

What is needed to convert evil and hate into good and compassion? How can we translate external limitations into the reality of achievement and personal fulfillment, embracing the notion that there need not be restraints on who we become and what we accomplish? How can we stay focused on the interior self, help others in their own quest, and fulfill our potential as enlightened, caring and complete individuals?

Thankfully, in this book our lessons come with the added virtue of being enjoyable. These are practical and amusing aphorisms that often leave you wondering, "did he really say that," even as you shake your head and smile. And yes, he really does say these things—often and repeatedly—all the while shifting between broad grins and fatherly admonitions.

Robert has said that an individual cannot expect the world to change, but we can change ourselves to follow basic principles of good that will make this world a better place. Implicit in this is the belief that we should live a fruitful, caring life; that we are a product of the choices we make; and where we end up is based on the path we take through the circumstances of our life.

This is the message of Robert Fisch, whose life is one that highly values the interior self and the individual's potential for self-fulfillment. He has not forgotten or totally erased any part of his life experience. Instead, he has let all of it shape and transform his person into a unique and extraordinary human being. He wishes the same for every other person.

Decades after emerging from the unfathomable horrors of the Holocaust and the later suppression of Communism in Hungary, he was interviewed by Phil Bosta for *Jewish Magazine*. His words remain relevant and important today:

"I subtitled my first book *A Lesson of Love from the Holocaust* because the Holocaust teaches us that good can be learned from even the worst human tragedies. It is not the ugliness of hate but the beauty of love that survives. What I would like to be remembered is not the horror, but the beauty created by human virtue and that the spirit can be enlightened even in the midst of suffering."

Robert would abhor the notion that this is a self-help book. View it instead as a flow of knowledge and life's lessons, delivered through very personal words and thoughts, from someone who has traveled a long and remarkable road. From it, we can gain insights into building our own lives with a sense of fulfillment, compassion and unrestrained potential. In that way, this most light-hearted and useful of the five books by Dr. Fisch may help each of us transform ourselves into equally humane "Happily Ever Afters."

– William W. McGuire, M.D.

Introduction

With reference to the ancient Chinese curse "I wish you an interesting life," I'd say that I've had *a hell of an interesting one*. I was a Jew during Fascism, a bourgeois under Communism, a rebel defeated in an uprising, a refugee among the free and a have-not amid plenty. I practiced medicine for nearly five decades in two countries, tending not only to the physical and emotional well-being of thousands of children but also to their preparation for the future. These experiences gave me witness to the physical, mental and emotional manifestations of life of many people from different backgrounds. My learning from experience is expressed in this book.

I do not think my parents planned for my birth. I was likely an accident, and most of the important happenings of my life were unplanned as well. When I first arrived in New York City, for example, someone showed me a map of the United States and asked where I wanted to go. With no knowledge, I pointed to Minneapolis and there I went.

Many years later, after an illustration of mine appeared in a local newspaper, a principal invited me to speak at her school. On the first evening, I talked with seven parents in a small library. I told them, among other things, that I was living in Budapest during

World War II, and at first I had been afraid of the Allies' air raids on that city. But then Germany occupied Hungary, and I learned that the Nazis were set on eliminating all the Jews. From then on, I did not care about the Allies' bombs. In fact, I thought of each one as bringing me closer to my ultimate survival.

After my speech, a man stood up and said, "I am so grateful to you." A bombardier over Budapest, he had always felt guilty about killing innocent people. A visiting Danish student whose grandparents had smuggled Jews to Sweden said something similar. The principal told me: "Your stories have such an impact. Why not write a book?"

On another occasion, when I was taking a course in a synagogue, I noticed a pleasant-looking woman, not only because she was attractive but also because her comments and ideas closely paralleled my own. One night after class, I asked her to join me for dinner at a nearby delicatessen. We had an animated conversation and after we finished our meal, I asked whether I could see her again. She answered, "I'm sorry, but I can't. I'm a nun, and I'm leaving next week for Rome."

These and all my other odd but informative experiences have resulted in a very personal philosophy:

• Suffering has made me realize what is important, what my values are. Hardship makes every minute beyond it all the more precious. I am grateful for even the smallest things life has given me.

• We must retain our humanity—our compassion for others—in every circumstance, no matter how brutal. We are all more alike than we are different, and each of us deserves the opportunity to fulfill our potential. We cannot correct one injustice by committing another but must treat others the way we want them to treat us.

To become humane, children must learn the value of a moral life and respect for others from an early age. No technical advancement will ever replace parental love, attention and education.

We live in an unusual time in which individual rights seem to supersede the good of society. Humanity, moral values and appropriate behaviors are restricted topics in our schools. In school, teachers and students may not even express their feelings with a hug.

• Health is a balance of physical, spiritual and emotional well-being—an index based upon satisfaction with ourselves, our relationships with others and their reflection upon us. Likewise, health is a gift of being aware, being free. We accept the universe for both its greatness and unimportance.

• Freedom—independence and the courage to break with the restrictions of convention—requires responsibility and self-reliance. It demands that we ask questions, make choices, take risks and accept consequences. It questions authority. If I always followed the rules, I would have died long ago.

Many people do not choose freedom over following the leader, and they often follow blindly, expecting things to be provided for them in return. I believe the individual can decide what is right for himself.

• Humor—the best way to make life palatable—is the ability to look at the funny, not the dark side of what is happening. I take it seriously!

• The beauty of art and music, more than anything else, brings spiritual dimension to our lives.

• No matter what we do, everything in the universe constantly changes. The only things we can change are ourselves.

That, in a nutshell, is my philosophy. The aphorisms and illustrations that follow are the simple and maybe amusing expressions of my observations, feelings and ideas after eighty-eight years on this planet.

Take what you like and leave the rest. And above all, enjoy.

– Robert O. Fisch

"Why do you stand there speechless and shudder?
Do you see life as a tragedy?
Look at it as comedy and be amused."

– Madách Imre
Hungarian poet

The Sky Is Not the Limit

Art

The first time I saw a painting of olive trees by Vincent van Gogh, I sat and shivered—overcome by the artist's genius. When I finished my training in pediatrics, I studied drawing and painting at night school for ten years, painting for fun. My daughter, at about the age of five, sat in my lap and together we painted huge flowers.

Art always has been a way for me to express feelings, to connect with my inner world and to escape reality. Initially I covered canvases with bright colors. More recently, I've realized my thoughts are better conveyed in black and white, with the simplest lines and forms. In this book and others I've written, I found myself author and illustrator. Art is communication; and for me, it is heartfelt, necessary and joyful.

Creation is the ultimate, ecstatic human experience.

Art takes us into another dimension, where justice and beauty prevail.

Art is a tangible manifestation of the human spirit.

Art relieves human suffering. It is an alternative medicine.

Art is an expression of the joy of being alive, a victory over mortality.

Art provides an appreciation for beauty, color, form and sound.

Art is a reflection of time.

Creation is the highest reward of the artist.

In art, the creation—not its permanence—is important.

In works of art and in genetic distribution, some are deficient, most are average and a few are exceptional.

Real art survives creators and critics.

Every great art was new once, but not every new art will be great.

Music transports one from a physical to a spiritual world.

Art is the highest form of human achievement.

Colors are the alphabet of joy.

Music has limitless influence
everywhere and through all time.

The lasting sculpture from marble
and the temporary sculpture of ice
spring from one artistic desire.

Colors are the notes of a
visual symphony.

Facing an empty canvas is
thrilling for the artist; there is
infinite possibility.

Without that first idea,
nothing follows.

Life and Death

As a young Jew in Hungary during the Second World War, I was destined for extermination by the Nazis. I saw hundreds of men and women tortured and shot and more who starved to death. In a distinctly different circumstance for me—as a physician, witnessing dying was not a rare experience.

Generally people consider serious illness, accidents and even death as tragically unexpected events. Not me. I believe life is a miracle, a never-repeated opportunity. But life, like everything else, comes with its pluses and minuses. It is neither perfect nor permanent, only transient. Aware of life's limits, I want to use every minute fully and happily.

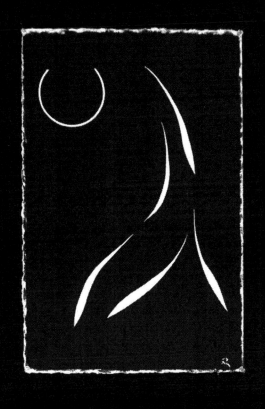

At the end, look not with sorrow but with joy at what has happened.

Life is the most precious gift we ever receive or give.

We are all subject to the laws of the universe, whereby change is constant and all form of life is impermanent.

Life is a one-way street.

Life may be extendable, but it is not permanent.

Suffering is one condition of life. Nights are long, but life is short.

Every second is a once-in-a-lifetime experience.

Life is like a piece of rubber string. Pulling at it extends each stage—childhood, adulthood and old age—but its substance remains the same.

To be or not to be? Dead is the question.

The meaning of life comes from living it fully.

Life is nanosecond awareness in the eternal darkness.

Who lives in the past misses the present.

More and newer problems arise with prolonged life.

Death is an incurable hereditary condition.

The loss of human lives cannot be measured in mathematical terms.

Once we accept limitations, all our relationships and experiences are precious and fulfilling.

Death is the only justice; no one is exempt.

We are all subject to the same physical and biological laws.

The end of one form of existence is the beginning of another.

As each passing day brings us closer to the end of life, the young and healthy among us are ignoring the transience of human existence.

We are wise to consider our inevitable death positively rather than negatively.

People usually dislike funerals, especially the last one—their own.

Don't think about how to die but how to live.

If we live well, our children and friends will look at the sky on starry nights and remember us not with sorrow for untold stories but with joy and gratitude for the beautiful words, songs and memories we left behind.

Inability or unwillingness to accept the inevitable opens the door to unhappiness.

Death cannot be taken lightly; the same can be said for the challenges of life.

Don't worry about what was or what will come; instead fully use present time. It is a gift that will never return.

When you look back, remember the beauty.

Life is full of problems, with occasional intermissions.

Make sure that when you reach the end of your days, you will have done the right things for yourself and others.

Send your messages before it is too late.

Look on life not as time decreasing but as experience increasing.

Emotions

Human emotions are the same. They are what they were; they are what they will be. The only difference in emotions today or fifty years ago, in this country or across the ocean, is the way they are expressed. Stereotypically, Italians are loud and gesture with their hands when expressing what they feel and think. Nordic Europeans hold back and stay quiet. Hungarians cry, even when we are enjoying ourselves.

At times, man is like a piece of wood, just flowing as the river takes us. Other times, we have choice. The direction is ours. That's when we should use words carefully. There is no more authentic, effective communication. Our energy—our emotions—help or hurt. Our emotions arc ours, the best gifts we share when bringing interest, kindness and warmth to the people we touch.

Peace of mind is the harmony between one's inner and outer worlds.

Feelings and thoughts are like the universe. They have no limits.

We have an inherent desire to be known and heard.

Expressing emotion is easier than controlling it.

We have to modify our feelings and relations with others to avoid conflict.

Real joy comes not to the individual alone but from that which is shared with others.

Bliss and depression are free of wishes.

We cannot fully appreciate joy without experiencing suffering.

Violence continues because hate and killing are biological instincts.

Suffering and deprivation can make us value the basic essentials of living.

Negative feelings poison thoughts, spoil personal relationships and reduce human involvement, productivity and joy.

It is frustrating when someone does not know how to do something. It is worse when someone knows what to do but is not allowed to do it.

Humor

Humor is my lifesaver. Most of the happenings around us take place without our control. If we are bitter, everything seems bad and dark. Humor changes the scene, opening the door to a different world. When a child eats chocolate, he ends up with a messy face. The chocolate smears on his fingers, mouth and chin make us laugh. When we drop chocolate on a white tablecloth, the mess makes us angry. The circumstance is the same; our response is different. Attitude makes all the difference in the world.

Depression is the worst manifestation of human moods. I know; I had it. When circumstances seemed hopeless, I became desperate. In a session with a psychologist, I complained nonstop. As the end of our hour drew close, he fell silent, then told me things would get worse. The thought was life-changing. My psychologist's sentence was similar to Buddhist wisdom: "Let things go." That was my reality check. Viewpoint is the difference, the miracle. I have learned to relax and enjoy life. Humor is the lens that works for me.

When a doctor said to a patient, "You are crazy," the patient asked for a second opinion. The doctor replied, "You are also ugly."

Don't look up to or down on people. Just laugh with them.

I often heard, "Kids are great." I thought they are small, but I came from a different country.

Better to be rich sooner than poor later.

Living well is better than a living will.

Maintaining an open-door policy is critically important for the restroom.

**Humor must be
taken seriously.**

**It's easy to like
everybody if you
exclude those
you hate.**

Some men suffer from
menstrual irregularities.

It could be worse, but not too much.

Past: The good news was that
the world was going in the right
direction; the bad news was that it
was moving slowly.
Present: The good news is that the
world is moving quickly; the bad
news is that it's moving in the wrong
direction.

The world has seven continents, but
countless people are incontinent.

Don't be pleased when a masochist
says, "I am so glad to see you."

Some people don't like nature, especially that of others.

The five senses do not include the common one.

More people make short stories long than long stories short.

Humor is a lifesaver.

When someone responds to "How are you?" with "So far I was well," it is not a compliment.

The most sexually transmitted condition is pregnancy.

An idea for eliminating waste: dry cleaning for disposable diapers.

A tumor is a space-occupying body. A pretty woman is a mind-occupying body.

Although families, neighbors and nations often do not talk with one another, we want to communicate with outer-space aliens.

If you answer the phone, you cannot say, "I am not here."

Veterinary hospitals with an arrow pointing in one direction for dogs and another for cats show clear evidence of discrimination.

Some lecture halls might do well to change "No Smoking" signs to "No Snoring."

Dating starts at birth.

"Justifying" the explanation follows every bad reaction.

Given that marriage of same-sex couples is now acceptable, isn't it time to reconsider polygamy?

A breakthrough in condoms is never popular.

If there is a "man for all seasons," there must be a "man for no reason."

People don't like to lose anything but their extra weight.

I asked a boy, "When is your birthday?" He answered, "Next year."

If driving cars causes global warming, then the lack of automobiles must have caused the Ice Age.

Some people say, "I don't remember. I have so much in my head." Most of them have limited storage.

Some same-sex couples are upset at not having the right to marry. Some married people, though unhappy in their own marriages, are upset that gay persons want to marry. Solution: eliminate marriage.

We forget more and more with increasing age; so that when we meet with God we will have nothing to complain about.

Our need to express ourselves is undoubtedly more important than our need to listen.

If God is on both sides, why is it necessary to fight?

Some people have "out-of-body" experiences. More have "out-of-mind" experiences.

Don't expect much of the blind man
who promises, "I'll look into it."

Infrequent is the statement, "Not
highly recommended."

Traveling alone never bores a good
conversationalist.

Where there's a whale, there's
a wave.

It's not the hair on the head
that matters, but the head
on the neck.

Good taste most likely costs more.

Sex is best when shared with another person.

The color of poisonous frogs is a warning. The color of sports cars is an invitation.

Some are neither affluent in finance nor fluent in English.

Those who talk to themselves have at least one attentive listener.

Please say stop if someone starts a story: "You will die when you hear this."

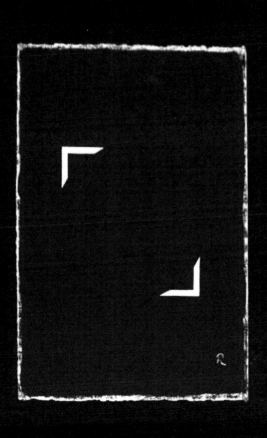

Dermatologists' interests must be skin-deep.

Ophthalmologists are unlikely to suggest that their patients participate in double-blind studies.

Ophthalmologists suggest that vitamin E is good for the eyes. Cardiologists found that vitamin E is bad for the heart. The truth is somewhere in between. If you take vitamin E, you will see death more clearly.

Some people are responsible for a co-pay, others for coping.

When they say he is not as bad as he looks, he might be worse.

What's new? Today.

During sex, if one is up and the other is down, is the couple bipolar?

Chocolate in small portions is poison; in large amounts a delicatessen.

If women did not oppose wearing veils, the cosmetic industry would be bankrupt.

Why do we say "highly" but never "lowly" educated?

If justice is served, why must one side appeal?

Is a parachute required for a pilot study?

Restaurants advertise happy hours between 4 and 6 p.m. Does that mean the other times are sad?

In a pilot study is visual acuity
a criterion?

Is it better to be killed by friendly fire
than by the enemy?

If you are frightened and nothing
happens, are you disappointed?

Is it bad to go to the Badlands?

Is it routine if someone doesn't
have one?

Why do we say "legally" rather than
"illegally" drunk?

How can we expect others to
understand us when we do
not know ourselves?

Sometimes a phone call is phony.

Do hot flashes contribute to
global warming?

Shouldn't target populations use
bulletproof vests?

Parents can choose their babies'
gender. Will the time come when
children can choose their parents?

If there are one-hand piano pieces,
why aren't there one-legged dances?

Should one ask the smiling pessimist, "What's wrong?"

Why do we need insurance to enter a hospital, rather than to leave it?

Should lions be concerned about their cholesterol levels?

When will restless mind syndrome be recognized?

Three be or not three be—why isn't that a question?

Why do flight attendants point out the life vests when we are flying over land?

Why is it called a "living will" when it is about dying?

Did Darwin mean the survival of the fittest or of the fetuses?

If someone hates everybody equally, can he be called a democrat?

If Mohammedans and Israelites dislike each another, is that anti-Semitism?

Did you ever hear anyone say, "I did my worst."?

Was Neil A. Armstrong a moon walker?

People are living longer than ever before. If someone meets an ancestor in heaven who died young, who has to be more respectful to the other?

People without mobility go nowhere.

If a kickback is unacceptable in business, why is it acceptable in athletics?

Love

L ove is an over-used word. How many times do you hear someone say, I love summer, modern art, baseball, National Geographic, ice cream, whatever? "Love" has become the casual alternative for what we like, admire, enjoy, collect or want.

I think real love is a rarity. For me, love is the fullness in my heart for those special people who by sheer strength of personality changed my life. They taught me what I needed to know and demonstrated values that I've adopted. There is no popularity contest. I am fortunate to have in my life maybe a dozen people who love me. They are the persons who understand my faults and eccentricities. I love them. They love me back, keep me strong and feed my soul. They make my life beautiful.

Dying from lack of love is worse than dying from disease.

Real love is unconditional.

Not the ugliness of hate but the beauty of love survives time.

If someone remains in only a single heart and mind, his life will have been worth living.

We must be careful to choose our words for the benefit of everyone.

Every day should be Valentine's Day.

Valuables are not what you leave in the bank but in human hearts and minds.

Love can be learned, even from hate.

Inner beauty,
relationships with
others and nature,
the ability to wonder
and enjoy special
moments—these are
within reach for people
at every age.

Humanity

All people are human, yet that doesn't necessarily translate to humane behavior. Bullying, jealousy, bigotry, crime, torture and war are epidemic among mankind. How many wars have been fought in the name of God? Is that humane?

I have been fortunate to know a number of persons who can easily be characterized as humane. During the Communist reign in Hungary, a doctor who was my superior invited me to his home. It was spare and modestly appointed. Next door was a large, beautiful, recreational building used as a vacation site, serving more than fifty government employees at a time. I wanted to know what the building was before the Communists' confiscation. He said it was his sanatorium. I asked, "Aren't you angry?" "No, Robert," he said. "Now many people can enjoy it." He had been robbed, but was forgiving and humane in his response.

Parents most often set examples for humane behavior, as do teachers, priests, rabbis and other clergy. They best model humanity by remaining humane in inhumane circumstances.

Real humanists find giving makes them richer.

Homo sapiens began when the four-legged first stood on two. Few stand up today even when necessary.

The joy of giving brings enlightenment.

Improve your life and the lives of others.

A good deed is better than a hundred promises.

Real friendship is not a give-and-take proposition.

Develop your potential.

**If we do not see identical
things the same way, how can
we expect to see different people
in identical ways?**

**The young people of today are
as sensitive, curious and open to
learning as those of the past. That
will be the same in the future.**

**We must take others into
consideration when choosing
to speak.**

**We should find the time, courage and
opportunity to understand others and
help them to understand us.**

Remain humane even in inhumane circumstances.

Humanity is not hereditary. It must be learned.

Given our limitations, how can we expect perfection?

Justice and fairness do not exist in biology.

A double standard is the biggest threat to civilization.

Don't expect rights without responsibility.

We emphasize human rights, but we can't neglect to mention human wrongs.

Mankind is a new species. It may take billions of years more to lose its animal instincts.

Einstein could not keep his thoughts
without paper and pen.

We all depend on each other.

Places are different, but people are not.

There is one percent difference
between the DNA of chimpanzees and
humans. What a difference
that makes!

We all use the same letters of the
alphabet, but the genius creates
masterpieces while others paint
vulgarities on walls.

Each of us is a unique,
unprecedented experiment
of nature.

One injustice cannot correct another.

The meanings for "we" and "they" are unbridgeable. This is language learned early. Say "we" and the others guys are bad guys for one reason only: "they" are not us.

In nature, everything has its complement or antagonist, its predator or prey. But man's antagonist is man.

Stand up for your principles; your first compromise will lead to actions you regret.

Make building your children's character a priority.

The humanitarian acts of individuals outshine brutality's darkness.

Those who fail to stand against tyranny become its victims or allies.

The bell-shaped curve
applies to every human
circumstance. No
religion, nation or race
is exempt from extreme
elements on each side
of the curve.

Human physical and
emotional needs never
change.

Think of yourself as a thread in a colorful carpet. Without the thread, there is no carpet; and without the carpet, the thread has no function. Your existence means nothing without others.

Being a victim does not qualify one as a judge.

Education, compassion and hard work provide hope that future generations will live in a better world.

None of us has a superior or inferior role. We have different ones.

History

Historians estimate fifty-nine million people were killed during the Second World War. I was fortunate to be liberated from the Gunskirchen concentration camp on May 4, 1945. After the war, my hatred of the Germans was simple, "I will kill them all." However, the first German I encountered when I was a free man was dirty and begging for food. I had to make a choice. I gave him food.

The Second World War ended. Wars didn't. Atrocities continue, terrorists attack, drones are dispatched to surprise and kill. It takes little for mankind to be reckless, greedy, uncomprehending, unfeeling and stupid.

When will human nature change? What can an individual do? One answer: Understand that what may be good for one person is bad for another.

When family members cannot get along with each other, why should we expect anything different from castes, nations, religions and races?

There is no evidence that people have become more tolerant or less greedy.

History is the result of human emotion, conflict and interest.

Don't believe your enemy's enemy is your friend.

For war: pit one president against the other to fight, one to one. Think of how many lives would be saved.

The yellow stars sewn on their clothes tattooed the victims inside.

World peace can be achieved only if the entire world population practices the same moral values. That is unlikely until mass destruction opens the minds of the few remaining survivors.

Every regime failed when the accepted laws and customs were not followed.

Revolution is like a river. After a flood, the river returns to its bed. It goes from one extreme to another.

In tyranny, fear, suspicion and distrust rule. Thieves and murderers are rewarded, and liars spread the gospel of hate.

The past is the past. Victims and their murderers have all become dust. Only justice is left.

The most dangerous people are the indifferent ones.

What we call a terrorist, the other side calls a freedom fighter.

We must take a stand against suppression and injustice.

It's easier to destroy a dictatorial system than to build a democratic one.

The Holocaust is not humanly comprehensible.

In the concentration camps, lipstick served not for making lips more exciting. It was used for its flavor, making lips less hungry.

Teaching humanity to children with the Holocaust as an example is like finding light in the darkness.

A real leader is the visionary who opens new doors for a better future.

Peace cannot be based on military strength alone. It requires understanding, compromise and compassion.

Liberation is the first step, but it takes at least two generations to achieve freedom.

Freedom is like a seedling reaching for the light.

Even those who never experience freedom seek it.

Freedom is the earthly equivalent of Nirvana, but heaven is not everyone's preference.

Political correctness is a way to silence those who oppose change that is motivated by politics rather than traditional values.

Those who enjoy freedom must extend it to others.

Those born free think little about their good fortune, just as one does not appreciate health until losing it.

As the suffering of an oyster produces beautiful pearls, so the Holocaust produced its heroes— not only among the victims and survivors but also among those who risked their lives to help and save the persecuted.

Those who achieve freedom feel like a climber reaching the summit of a mountain.

Many people do not choose freedom. It requires responsibility and self-reliance.

Freedom depends on internal and external factors.

After they left office, recent presidents built libraries. Unfortunately, as presidents they didn't build the country.

Freedom is more than a lack of fear.

Political correctness is politic, without value or permanence. What is considered politically correct today was neither political nor correct in the past, nor will it be in the future. It's like confusing hypocrisy for democracy.

Wisdom
and Values

Wisdom and values are inseparable. One without the other is like an open circle. I learned early about human values because, quite simply, that's our connection to each other. As a boy, I observed my father, always ready to help others. He wasn't critical of those in need, he didn't seek compensation for what he did; he did what was right because it never crossed his mind that there was an alternative. Generosity, trust, loyalty and respect are the core values that undergird any wisdom I've gained.

Anna, the nanny who raised me, was crippled and barely able to walk when I was sent to a work camp. Pitted against the horror of war, she limped to a barbed wire barricade, bribed a guard and brought me, among other things, a blanket that kept me warm until the end of the war. That blanket was treasure, and Anna's effort is still a touchstone for me nearly seventy years later.

I think the most important value is the regard we can show one another—even for a second, even in hardship. Finding the positive side of life and sharing that with others is the value that endures.

A B C D E F G H

J K L M N O P Q R

S T U V W X Y Z

Simple communication is the most effective communication.

You cannot change the world. You can change yourself and maybe a few others.

It is impossible to observe reality without changing it.

The world has been changing for billions of years regardless of the existence of mankind.

We are less aware of what is going on inside of us than what is going on around us.

The person who caused an accident describes it differently than the persons who experienced or witnessed it.

What we are conscious of is
not even the tip of an iceberg.
It is an incomprehensibly tiny
manifestation of our underlying,
immense unconscious.

Hold onto what is still within
reach, and let go of what is
attainable no more.

There is no one-sided coin.

Light comes from the sun. Brilliance
is seen in smart men and women.

Even an ignorant person can be right.

In order to see, open your eyes. In
order to understand, open your mind.

The spherical has no sides.

Wise persons listen more than
they talk.

Luck is useful, but determination is
more effective in attaining goals.

A little sunshine makes the difference
between day and night.

Those who question the existence
of other life in the universe err like
those who believed the Earth is at
its center.

A straight line is the shortest—but
not necessarily the fastest—way
between two points.

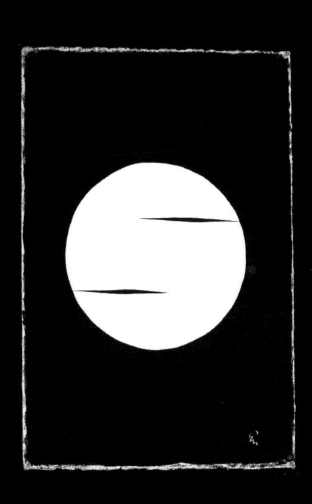

Under the laws of the universe, change is constant and all forms of existence are contingent.

Children are not born good. They are born innocent.

There are differences between humans and animals. There is more killing among the humans who are not seeking food.

In the universe there are no directions, top or bottom, left or right.

The biggest risk is not to take any.

We must alter our biologically enforced attitudes with broadly accepted civilized laws and customs.

Whatever individual abilities are determined by inheritance, no one can achieve his or her potential without emotional and intellectual support from others.

The real dreamer doesn't need a bed.

The ignorant are those who do not want to learn.

Time has quickly changed the outside world, but inside we have changed very little.

A double standard is always damaging.

We make some selections unconsciously, the choice based upon our previous experience and preference.

Some suffer acrophobia when looking down, yet we experience no space phobia when looking up at the vast night sky.

There is no good solution among bad situations.

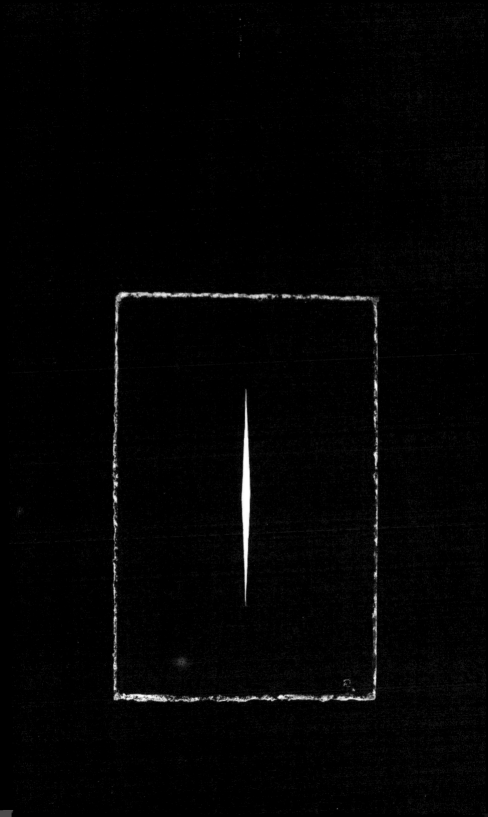

We think we alter nature, but nature really alters us.

There is no beginning or end—only continuity.

Nothing and no one can stay on top permanently.

Survival requires sacrifice.

Life is like mountain climbing: when you reach one peak, there is always another peak even higher.

In recent decades, student achievement did not improve across the board because we paid more attention to the poorly performing students. We did not give equal support to all children.

Law cannot keep up with scientific progress.

Deviations from average
(normal) are considered abnormal.
Yet extremes may be rewarded
or punished.

Changes are not necessarily better or
worse but different and inevitable.

See more, hear more, read more,
learn more. The mind has no
boundaries.

Titles should be used not only for
privilege but also for obligation.

A lot of muscle cannot solve a
little puzzle.

A double standard is no standard.

The middle road is typically the safest and the least exciting.

The wise person wants to know more.

Do not be sorry about what you do not have anymore. Be happy you once had it.

A killer whale can't communicate to another in the same school.

Surfaces fade first.

The worst defeat is not trying.

For a pioneer, even failure has merit.

A fundamental value is not the beautification of skin and hair but the enrichment of the spirit and mind.

Our stomachs urge us to eat more and more, while our educated brains coax us to eat less.

Being genetically programmed to eat to store and conserve energy, we tend to move in energy-saving ways.

The real problem is not lack of available resources but the rapidly growing population.

If someone stops growing, he stops living.

If we knew what we don't know, we would be much smarter.

Even smart people must take a chance sometimes.

Most actions and material existences eventually fade away without leaving a trace.

Communication is the most powerful, natural human tool.

Two snowflakes are not the same and neither are people.

We should provide equal opportunity for everyone; but those who study, work and show creativity deserve credit and greater reward.

No complicity exists without dependency and cooperation.

The joy of giving brings enlightenment.

Recognize opportunity. Act with willingness, ability and determination.

The lucky one is content with life.

The Author Himself

I live an interesting life. Some call it "colorful." A label is not important to me. Laughter is.

Happiness exists in the smallest thing; a slice of bread is a treat. Blue sky, soft rain, opera, a baby's smile and a phone call from someone I love are gifts. People often tell me I am an optimist. I am not really. Rather, I accept that everything changes and, therefore, anything I have is a blessing.

I believe that everything and all of us are a temporal part of something incomprehensibly large. I try to make the most of what life offers. I wish to share my thoughts and philosophy for others to laugh.

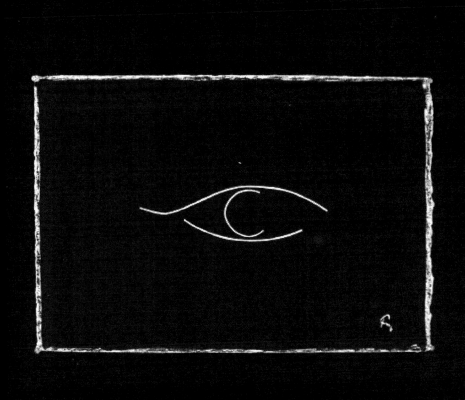

I know reincarnation exists. Looking in the mirror year after year, I see myself in different bodies.

A fish without a "c" is not a Fisch.

I have dubious titles—the best pediatrician among painters and the best-known painter among pediatricians.

Everyone has a shortcoming, but I have a lot of them.

I am a Hungarian-American or a hungry American.

People say, "I don't remember; I have so much in my head." I say, "It's because I have so little."

I am so clumsy that when I put my hands under a motion-sensitive faucet, no water flows.

Darwin was wrong. I'm proof of the survival of the unfit.

My life is so beautiful, it may be an illusion. When I die, I'll awake from the dream.

I don't know what I'm going to say, but I can barely wait to hear it.

I'm not impatient; I'm only in a hurry.

I respected the American soldiers who liberated me in the concentration camp as though they were my second parents. They renewed my life.

When I was born, my mother started a double-blind study: she loved my brother.

If I didn't forget so easily, I would have better memory.

Before I speak to an audience, I ask its members to tell me if they understand anything I say.

I am the only one who really understands me.

My mind is like my body, changing daily for the worse.

Suffering taught me to appreciate every moment of life.

I am not sorry for what I haven't had, but happy with what I have.

If someone said, "I love you." I'd say, "Me, too."

I sold my soul very cheaply to the devil. He made the worse deal.

I have permanent tinnitus (ear ringing). If I am not hearing, I think I am either more deaf or no one cares to call me anymore.

I have a special
obligation to show
that my life is more
than survival.

Everyone can do one thing better than anyone else—read his own handwriting. I am the exception.

I have one agreement with my wife. We do not agree on anything else.

I wouldn't start a new life. I would just continue my current one.

I answer even before I hear the question.

I am always right except when I am wrong.

I came from an extinguished family.

Following my colonoscopy at age eighty-one, the doctor asked me to return in ten years. I asked, "In the morning or the afternoon?"

Aging

Life is that time—positive, challenging, negative—between birth and death. In the United States in the middle of the eighteenth century, life expectancy was about forty years; today it tips beyond eighty. And change is the constant in our appearance, physical well-being, relationships and interests. Fighting the inevitable is a time-wasting, loser's battle.

Longevity is hollow compared to happiness. I am convinced that the older we get and the less we expect, the more we have. That's the beauty of aging.

It is the quality of life not the length of time that matters.

Wouldn't it be better to start life by emerging from the grave and end it by disappearing into the womb?

Age should not decrease but increase the value of joy.

Some people show rapid signs of gradual aging.

Each period of life has advantages and disadvantages.

Adolescents' problems usually come to an end; teenagers grow up.

"Long time" is in the terminology of the finite, not of the infinite.

In old age, the main issue is not how things could be better but how to live with things as they are.

Every day is special.

It's a myth that old people can't do things faster than young ones; for example, they forget faster and die sooner.

We are on a moving belt. Some get on while others get off.

**Yesterday is past.
Tomorrow is a wish.
Today is the only
time in which to do
something.**

**There are no
appropriate measures
for eternity.**

As we cannot sense the motion
of the Earth, we cannot sense the
passage of time.

The person who stops growing
assumes a living death.

Negative feelings decrease both the
quality and quantity of time.

Older people talk to themselves
because they can do so without a
hearing aid.

Immortality is the most impossible
and undesirable wish.

Adolescence is a reverse
metamorphosis in which butterflies
temporarily become worms.

With positive acceptance of the limits of time, relationships and experiences become more precious and fulfilling.

When you have too many problems, time seems limited. When you have too much time, your problems increase.

Young people face many unanswered questions. As they grow older, most of the questions remain. Later they forget the questions.

The deterioration of a man's outsides is inevitable, but improvement inside is possible.

A fourteen-year-old thinks a person of thirty is very old. The eighty-year-old thinks a person of seventy is very young.

Only the sick and the old are aware of the transience of human existence.

With old age comes a biological change. What previously was soft becomes hard and vice versa.

Awareness of time is the recognition of its limits.

It's not a compliment to be told one hasn't changed with age. It is an insult.

Someday the baby pictures will be antiques.

One advantage to being old is that you don't have to start all over again.

Getting older doesn't necessarily mean getting wiser.

Some older persons complain about short-term memory loss, others about long-term memory loss. The rest do not know what any of them are talking about.

The only way to prevent aging is to die young.

The reason for longevity remains secret because those who have lived long have forgotten it.

If someone wants to live forever, ask him, "What would be your plan for 3 p.m. on June 12, in the year 2,874,963,120,023?"

Advanced age is mostly the result of changes in social and environmental improvements, and partly the result of medical advancements.

One of the advantages of old age is that it does not last long.

The only "opportunity of a lifetime" is this moment.

At an advanced age, not being sick is pathological.

Both the young and the old are ignorant. The young ones have not learned enough; the old ones have forgotten too much.

The past, like a shadow, accompanies us to the grave.

An elderly person can be happy just because he remembers why he goes into another room.

In the past, wisdom was considered part of old age. These days senility most likely comes with old age.

Learning has no age limit.

Marriage
and Family

I grew up in a small, loving family: mother, father and older brother. We knew both happy and horrible experiences, the latter due in large part to our religion, nationality and the times. My mother wanted my brother and me to have all that she missed as a child. My father, joyful and generous, lived as though life was an operetta and died the suffering, prolonged death common in operas.

When I became a father, my world turned inside out. The birth of my daughter changed my perspective; she was beautiful beyond what I felt I deserved. Every day became extraordinary. I started to see things through her eyes. That innocence and wonder refreshed my soul. And taunted me, too. Nothing has been more important to me than my daughter's readiness for a productive and happy life. I knew she would eventually learn what I knew: life comes with ups and downs. Laughs do not come without tears.

It is a parent's responsibility to provide for their children. Schools will never replace the first years of parental care and love. A rabbi told me the three most important things for a parent to provide their children are example, example and example.

Same-sex couples should have the same rights as heterosexual couples. But their union should not be called marriage. Look what happened to the word "gay." The word "marriage" deserves a better future.

Those who divorced never want to have more experience with wild life.

A good marriage requires both partners to maintain their individuality.

The Hubble telescope shows that the galaxies are moving farther and farther apart. A similar statement could be made about many married couples.

A child's early education starts with the parents.

We are who they were, and they will be us.

No school can replace parental love, care, example and encouragement.

Early *Homo sapiens* did not practice divorce because it was not possible to divide a cave.

Abortions and sexual preferences are not national but personal choices, and should remain that way.

In some marriages, the best thing was the divorce.

A newborn's mother prefers an invisible heart lesion for her baby rather than a noticeable cleft lip.

Being alone can be lonely, but it is worse to be with someone and feel lonely.

"Better than nothing" cannot be said of some divorces.

An engaged couple might take more than a year to plan their wedding after having talked for only an hour or so about what it means to spend their life together.

Religion

Since the time of cave dwellers, man has looked for that special something missing on Earth. The something that prompted creation, that made the stars, flowers, seasons—the something that holds the secrets, magic and mystery of life. Scientists proffer theories. To explain the unexplainable, many look to religion.

I was a religious Jewish child, raised by a Catholic nanny. I respect every religion. Yet I am and always will be a Jew. This is my destination, not by choice but by circumstance. But as my hair has changed from black to gray, my faith more strongly embraces human responsibility. My religion is "treat others as you want to be treated and approach life with reverence."

For most people, religion is the first step toward enlightenment.

Man can't criticize the way God made heaven, but God may certainly have reservations about some of His creations on Earth.

God's law is good for humanity, but His indifference to enforcement is questionable.

Few humans are able to reach heaven on Earth, so they wish to be there after death.

Is a hearing deficit an advantage when the Lord calls?

Did the imagination of man create God, or did the imagination of God create man?

Medicine

In medical school in Hungary, I saw children in the isolation wards, where their parents were not allowed to go. Nothing touched me more than the tears of helpless sick children, crying to be hugged and kissed.

At the University of Minnesota, where I started my pediatric training, I was asked to care for severely retarded babies. They had been born with an inherited metabolic disease called phenylketonuria (PKU).

While this suffering was different than what I'd known as a teenager, this was a war of sorts for me. PKU was genetic, and the human tragedies were similar. And so, too, were glimmers of hope.

Over time, the uncle of one of my patients discovered the way to screen newborns for PKU. With early dietary treatment they develop normally. I documented previously unknown consequences of PKU, and for the first time suggested and proved that PKU mothers without dietary restrictions could produce normal healthy infants by a gestational carrier.

Medicine is a profession where the ultimate aim is unachievable. No one lives forever. Often, however, life can be improved, prolonged and enjoyed. That goal fills my heart.

In medicine a final victory cannot be claimed. Doctors transform one problem into another, winning battles but losing the war.

When doctors reach the end of medical resources, they feel a mixture of frustration and powerlessness. They search for answers that their knowledge fails to provide.

The conflict between the mind and the body has increased.

Statistical probabilities alone are not enough to help patients.

The doctor examining a new patient is as challenged as the artist starting a new work.

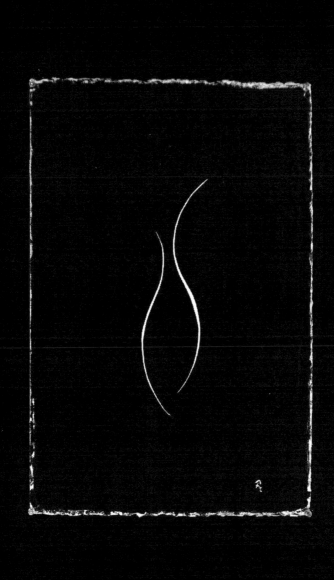

Medicine and art are inseparable.

Art and medicine are two consequences of the desire to sustain life.

It's easier to read a doctor's mind than his handwriting.

Nature discriminates. Some diseases occur more in one group than another.

Restoration artists are similar to doctors. Both repair damaged products.

All medical advice is good; the art is to give it to the right patient.

Some doctors pretend rather than attend.

I asked one patient whether his hernia was incarcerated. He said, "No, I was."

Physicians can make patients feel better and live longer—but only to a certain point. If we think of our existence in this context, then we can wisely consider our inevitable, individual death a positive rather than a negative phenomenon.

Doctors are obliged to offer patients—young and old, curable or incurable, hopeful or hopeless—not only the most appropriate diagnostic and therapeutic procedures but also to help with the time left to them.

Doctors cannot provide optimal care for patients if they ignore everything except the direct cause and effect of the disease.

Doctors must consider the complexity of biological, mental and environmental factors.

If it's a penny for your thoughts, why do psychiatrists charge so much?

Why don't we call fertility doctors "godfathers"?

Proctologists do not see light at the end of the tunnel.

Another doctor said to a pathologist, "And what is new on the other side of the Rubicon?"

Does the semi-retired surgeon cut back?

There is no cure for medicine.

A misleading doctor might be called a con-doctor.

Approximately forty percent of patients fail to take medications as prescribed. No wonder the medications for memory loss seem ineffective.

Doctors should give outstanding rather than standing orders.

Suggestion for a prescription bottle: "Use until the rash, the medication or the patient is gone."

A hospital is a repair shop.

The worst phobia is the fear of life.

When a doctor's phone rings, a patient may be dying to hear from him.

Radiology clinic signs read: "If you are pregnant, notify the technician." How about putting a sign in the infertility clinic: "If you are not pregnant, notify the technician."

As life expectancy increases, more
new diseases will appear.

The worst clinic scenario is not when
a patient arrives in bad shape, but
when he leaves that way.

A hypocritical oath cannot replace
the Hippocratic one.

"Routine visit" is the medical term for
maintenance service.

Even the friends of a pathologist
never ask him, "Would you check
me out?"

Living is an art, and
medicine makes life a little
better and longer.

The Sky Is Not the Limit.

The Grave Is.

Photo by Siari & Forrai Photography

Robert O. Fisch is a native of Budapest, Hungary, and a survivor of the Holocaust. Following World War II, he returned to Hungary and completed medical school. In 1956 he was an active participant in the revolution against Communist suppression. After Dr. Fisch escaped from Hungary, he became a medical intern at the University of Minnesota and was a professor of pediatrics there from 1979 until his retirement in 1997. Dr. Fisch is known internationally for his clinical research in phenylketonuria (PKU), a genetic disease. For his heroism, the Hungarian government awarded him a medal in 1995 and knighthood in 2000.

An award-winning artist, Dr. Fisch studied at the Academy of Fine Arts in Budapest, Minneapolis College of Art and Design, University of Minnesota and Walker Art Center. Dr. Fisch's first book, *Light from the Yellow Star: A Lesson of Love from the Holocaust,* is an eloquent portrayal of his Holocaust experience. His message focuses on the importance of the human spirit and love that led the way for survivors. The original paintings with the text have been exhibited in the United States, Europe and Israel, and the book itself is widely distributed in schools in the United States [by the Yellow Star Foundation (yellowstarfoundation.org)] and Hungary.

Dr. Fisch wrote and illustrated *The Metamorphosis to Freedom* as a testimonial to freedom, the value he treasures above all others. Having survived the two most oppressive regimes of the 20th century, he is eminently qualified to write and speak about the quest for freedom. *Dear Dr. Fisch: Children's Letters to a Holocaust Survivor* is a collection of letters selected from thousands Dr. Fisch received from American and European students who heard his message. Their letters are filled with love, humor, idealism, common sense and gratitude. *Fisch Stories – Reflections on Life, Liberty, and the Pursuit of Happiness,* illustrated by the author, is historical and philosophical, funny and solemn, humane and barbaric, realistic and sentimental. Each story portrays the presence of humane values.